Ripley and Send

THEN AND NOW

The Changing Scene
of
Surrey Village Life

Newark Priory.

Send & Ripley History Society
Surrey

The cover photograph is a haymaking scene
from 1931. Joe Baigent (on the left) and
Walter Giles are seen enjoying a break
in a hayfield off Send Road, now
the Sandfields Estate.

ISBN 0 9509961 0 6

Typeset and Printed by Lyndhurst Printing Company Limited,
Hardley Industrial Estate, Hythe, Southampton SO4 6ZX

Printed in England

Foreword

Most of us mourn the passing of what we once knew — empty fields now occupied by homes, old buildings pulled down to make way for development, long-established social patterns disrupted. Yet it is as well to remember that the old itself was once the new and that our forebears were not always fastidious in the changes they wrought; conservation is a relatively modern concept. Moreover adaptation to new circumstances is vital for successful survival. It is the rapidity and scale of change as well as insensitivity to the environment which often makes it so difficult to come to terms with new developments.

It would be regrettable just to let the past fade and die without recording for posterity the contributions made by previous generations to the life of our historic parishes. The way of life of each generation, as it is expressed by its material surroundings, is a fit and fascinating study for those that follow. The 16th and 17th Centuries may seen remote to us today, but we are fortunate that many buildings of those periods, and earlier, survive in this area and contribute to the richness of the environment in which we live.

With all signs indicating a quickening in the pace of social change into the foreseeable future, Send & Ripley History Society, in producing a publication illustrating so graphically the developments within our communities during the 19th and 20th Centuries, is rendering an inestimable service to us all. By focusing on a 'then-and-now' theme for this photographic presentation, the Society has evocatively captured the changing scene of two thriving Surrey villages which should appeal to resident and visitor alike.

Baden Powell

The Lord Baden-Powell
Chapel Farm
Ripley, Surrey.

Preface

It has been a privilege and pleasure to be associated with the production of this book, first and foremost to have worked with a most able and congenial sub-committee and secondly to have had an added opportunity to pursue my own special interest in photography.

This project was conceived by Send and Ripley History Society through its programme of preserving pictorial records from which a photographic archive is developing. The growth of these records has happily coincided with the steady accumulation of historical data based upon years of painstaking local research.

This resulting publication however could not have been produced without the support of the Society's members and friends and the devoted hard work of the committee.

It is therefore appropriate to commemorate the 10th anniversary of the founding of the Society by dedicating this book to its members and to everyone who has an interest in the history of the parishes of Send & Ripley.

K.H. BOURNE Msc.   Chairman

Send & Ripley History Society

Introduction

The earliest evidence of human occupation of the Send & Ripley area consists of struck flints left in the Neolithic period of 4000 to 2400 BC.

The first documentary evidence of Send occurs in an Anglo-Saxon land charter of 960-2 AD recording the sale of 20 hides of land at "Sendan" to Archbishop Dunstan of Canterbury for 90 pounds. The Domesday Survey of 1086 lists 15 slaves, 15 villagers and 26 smallholders, as well as a church, 2 mills and 5 fisheries. The figure of 20 hides is again mentioned. Ripley is first mentioned as "Rippelle" in a document of 1204.

The area covered remained substantially unchanged until 1984, when land south of Ripley by-pass was transferred to West Clandon. Within the original ancient parish of Send, Ripley separated ecclesiastically in 1878, and for civil purposes in 1933.

The chancel of Ripley Church, dated about 1160, is the oldest building in the ancient parish. Of exceptionally high quality, it was probably of monastic origin. Just before 1200, Augustinian Canons were given land to construct a priory which later became known as Newark. The Priory would have loomed large in the lives of local people since the manor of Ripley & Send was administered by the Prior for some 350 years until dissolution by Henry VIII in 1539.

The chancel of Send Church is dated about 1220, the church mentioned in Domesday being presumably then rebuilt in stone. A historical guide to this church has been published by Send & Ripley History Society.

The oldest domestic building so far identified is Vintage Cottage in Rose Lane, Ripley, built about 1400 on the open hall plan. In Send, Old Manor Cottage at Send Marsh, dated perhaps 1450, is believed to be the oldest. Many other timber-framed houses date from the great rebuilding of the 16th Century, and these, some of which appear in this book, help give the district its distinctive character.

As Henry VIII built up his fleet at Portsmouth greater traffic on the main road would have brought increased prosperity to Ripley. Likewise completion of the Wey Navigation over a century later in 1653 brought more trade to Send. In making the meandering River Wey navigable, initially from the Thames to Guildford, it gave Send a new de facto physical boundary.

The 1749 Turnpike Act to "Amend the road from Kingston to Petersfield" resulted in London to Portsmouth becoming a day's journey by stage coach whereas previously it had taken the coach a day to reach Guildford. The increased traffic brought further prosperity with Georgian houses, such as Ryde House, being built and others such as The Talbot and The Georgian House, being given their impressive facades.

As a result of the Inclosure Act of 1803, 1600 acres of common land were allotted to land owners. This included Burnt Common and Send Heath and paved the way for the development of Clandon Road, Cartbridge and Send Road. It spelled the end of many broad roadside verges but, fortunately, ensured the preservation of Ripley Green and Woking Broadmead.

Yet another factor which has changed the face of the area is mineral extraction. Send, as the name implies, has always been known for its sand and doubtless the building trade has taken advantage of its availability at all times. Extraction accelerated rapidly with increasing demand for concrete, making it arguably second only to agriculture as a local industry.

After the development of the turnpike road, the stage coach traffic reached its zenith in the early 1800s and the Victorian diarist, A.J. Munby, noted that, in the 1820's, there had been 27 coaches a day through Cobham. The completion of the railway to Guildford in 1845 and eventually to Portsmouth in 1859 for a time diverted traffic from the trunk road and Munby recorded that by 1863 there was but one carrier a week from London to Ripley.

The deserted "great white road" was tailor-made for the early bicyclists when the high bicycle ("penny farthing") was developed. From 1876 onwards they came in increasing numbers to Ripley and prosperity was restored. Motor transport began to replace the bicycle on the Ripley Road from the turn of the century bringing ever increasing congestion to Ripley. The opening of the by-pass in 1976 provided some relief until the general increase in traffic and the opening of the motorway at Wisley in 1983 began to bring it back again.

We think the reader of this book will find that despite the disappearance of, or change in, many old buildings, enough remains for an 18th Century traveller brought forward in time to recognise his surroundings. Long may it remain so, but constant vigilance is required.

L.G. Bowerman.

Acknowledgements

The task of producing this book was painstakingly undertaken by a small group of the Society's members:

Betty Pamplin photographed, processed and printed most of the present day views as well as reproducing some of the archival material.

Ken Bourne produced copies of most of the old and some of the new photographs and designed the front cover.

Duncan Jennings also produced some of the modern views and used his special expertise to create the front cover illustration.

The task of researching historical data and writing most of the text was carried out by Bette and John Slatford.

Bob Gale contributed additional text and was responsible for the layout.

Les Bowerman wrote the introduction and gave valuable guidance with the final editing.

Acknowledgement is also due to the many members and friends of the Society who gave help and advice and particularly to the following who loaned photographs for use in this book.

Mrs. Rita Avery
Messrs D. & P. Benzimra
Barretts Garden Buildings Ltd.
Mr. Ken Bourne
Mr. Les Bowerman

Mr. Roger Brown
Mrs. Dorothy Challen
Miss Dorothy Colborne
Mr. Peter Conisbee
Dr. Bob Gale

The late Mr. John Edden
Mr. John Dendy Evershed
Mr. Ken French
Mr. Reg Giles
Mrs. Alberta Giles
Mr. Stuart Groves
Mrs. Janet Hill
Mr. Lyn Mileham
Mr. Ken Methold
Mrs. Margaret Meech
Miss Betty Nokes

Miss Rose Onslow
Mrs. Doris Pullen
Mr. Geoff Pinnock
Mr. Jack Richardson
Mrs. Marjorie Sex
Mr. Peter Shoesmith
Mrs. Ivy Sopp
Mr. & Mrs. Ted Strange
Mrs. Joan Styles
Mr. Bill Titcombe
Mrs. Ivy Wilkinson

We also wish to thank the following organisations and individuals:

Surrey County Council, County Planning Office, for permission to reproduce photographs held in their archives.

Surrey Record Office, Guildford Muniment Room and Surrey Archaeological Society for assistance with historical research.

London Borough of Lambeth, Archives Dept. (Minet Library) for permission to reproduce water colours by J. and E. Hassell and H. Petrie.

The Rotary Club of Ripley and Send for permission to reproduce old views of Ripley from their collection.

Charles Thurbin for permission to photograph his model of Newark Priory.

The Imperial War Museum, Department of photographs.

The National Motor Museum, Beaulieu.

British Telecommunications for permission to reproduce the drawing of Richard Green's ironmongers shop.

IPC Business Press Ltd. For use of references from Kelly's Directories.

Special thanks are due to Phyllis Bourne. She endured interminable meetings in her home during the preparation of this book and provided us with endless supplies of coffee.

It is inevitable in a pioneering work of this kind that errors and ommisions will occur. We apologise for any that may be found in this book and hope that the reader will not hesitate to bring these to our attention.

" It seems as if in one were cast
The present and the imaged past,
Spanning, as with bridge sublime
That dreadful lapse of human time,
That gulf, unfathomably spread
Between the living and the dead."

Extract from "Newark Abbey", written in 1842,
by Thomas Love Peacock (1785 − 1866)

NB: Newark Priory is often mistakenly called Newark Abbey.

This model by Charles Thurbin is a conjectural reconstruction of Newark Priory as it may have appeared in the sixteenth century prior to the Dissolution. It is based upon the standing remains and a plan of the excavated foundations produced by Capt. C.M.H. Pearce (S.A.C. Vol. XL).

The principal remains of Newark Priory are the east end of the presbytery, part of the choir to the rear and the south transept (on the left of the photograph).

This estate agents map of the district dates from about 1927. Fruins probably did not remain in business under that name for much longer since Kelly's Directory of 1930 lists the firm as L. Fruin (Executors of) Estate Agent.

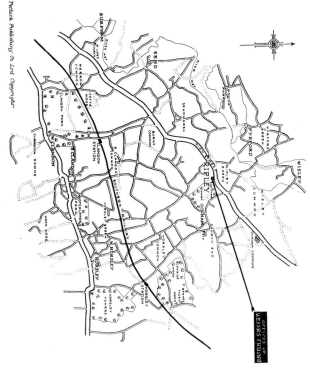

Ripley.

When entering Ripley from London this gateway is an impressive landmark though now sadly neglected. Formerly one of the entrances to Ockham Park it stands today forlornly isolated by the new A3 which passes a short distance behind. Much of the embellishment, including the overhead lamp, has now gone. Ockham Park, destroyed by fire in 1948, was the principal home of the first Earl and Countess of Lovelace (she was Lord Byron's daughter) before they moved to East Horsley in the 1840s.

Near the London end of Ripley High Street is Yew Tree House. Early this century it was the sanatorium for Ryde House School, founded in the 1860s by Thomas Marriott Berridge in the fine Georgian house of that name just opposite. The school later moved to the other end of the village. Yew Tree House is probably mid-eighteenth century.

Part of the building now Hartley Antiques was a bakery until 1963. From census returns and local directories of the last century it is known that a bakery was here in 1826 and that from then until at least 1867 it was run by a family named Hyde. The house, which is dated around 1700, has been much altered and extended in recent years, although the upstairs front is original.

Talbot Cottage, on the right, is slightly older as was its neighbour now demolished.

The Talbot Hotel features on many Ripley postcards both old and new. These views looking towards London emphasise the change in the scene due to the growth of the trees. The old view shows, on the left, Ryde House built in 1776 on the site of an earlier cottage which was encroached from Ripley Green.

High Street, Ripley.

W.H.A.
Photo Series. No. 557.

Looking towards Guildford, note the tall archway leading to The Talbot yard. In its heyday, during the coaching era, The Talbot was an important post-house on the Portsmouth Road. Although the front is mid-eighteenth century, the buildings behind, on the right, are for the most part of seventeenth century construction.

There was, however, probably an earlier building on the site, since it is known that a George Stanton kept the "Tabut" in the 1570s. He was regularly fined by the Manorial Court for "being a common innkeeper in Ripley and taking excessive profit."

The scene depicted on this 1823 J. Hassell drawing of the Talbot and the High Street is easily recognisable today. The little house to the right of the main building was the Talbot Tap. This was replaced in 1898 by a new Tap (bottom left) which, after fire damage in 1972, was itself rebuilt as an extension to the hotel (bottom right).

Standing by one of several entrances to Ripley Green, Elm Tree House has altered little between the times of these photographs. Long since a private house, it was listed in the census returns between 1851 and 1881 as a "seminary" for "ladies."

Ripley.

Looking up the High Street towards London, the principal change is the disappearance of "The Gables" on the right hand side. The first house on the right, of which part is now the chemist's shop, was until 1853 the White Horse Inn.

The modern Esso petrol station at the corner of White Horse Lane stands on the site of "The Gables" whose demolition in 1972 was the subject of considerable controversy. Petrol has been sold here for many years. "The Antiquities of Surrey" described "The Gables" as being sixteenth century.

Ripley would have witnessed military movement in times of international tension and war, even long before the motor car.

These pictures, taken by a local photographer, Mr Frank Pinnock, in the early part of the First World War, show military convoys in the High Street near the White Hart Inn.

The views include motor machine gun units riding Scott motor cycle and sidecar combinations, some with shields probably designed for the Vickers machine gun and others carrying ammunition boxes and tents. The waggons, pulled by mules, probably belonged to the transport section of an infantry division.

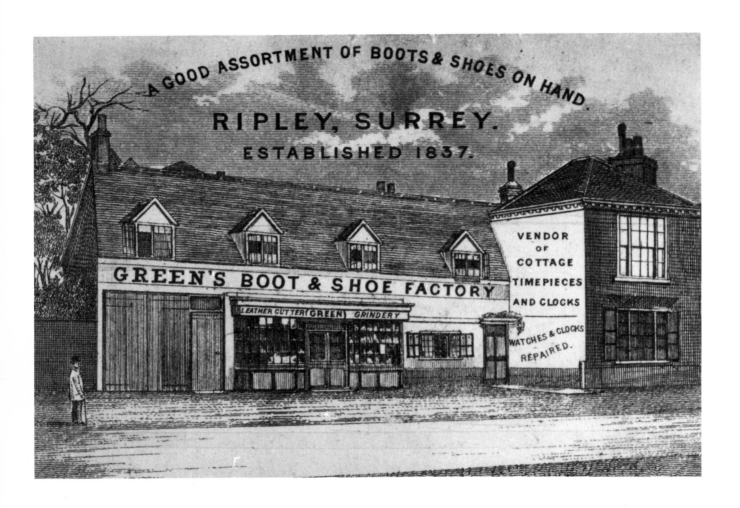

This business was established by Stephen Green who was one of a family of tally shoemakers (or cordwainers) selling their wares around the district. He later expanded into clothing, household goods, jewellery and ironmongery. The last became a separate business in the shop across the road in the name of his son Richard Green. Richard's son, William Bonfield, carried on the main business as W.B. Green and he was succeeded for a short time by his son Sidney before acquisition in 1935 by the father of the present owner, Mr. Bruce Wylie. Although the building has been considerably altered, the right hand upstairs window remains the same.

Richard Green's cycle and hardware shop, latterly owned by the Nokes family, was destroyed in a spectacular fire in 1969 and never re-opened. Modern houses were built in its place a few years later. The fire started when a paraffin tank on the upper floor over-flowed whilst it was being filled from a delivery tanker.

23

Looking along the High Street towards Guildford, probably in the 1920s, almost every building on the right has now disappeared for various reasons. The White Hart Inn, on the left, has recently closed. The water fountain by the side of the road has also gone, but it seems that no one is able to remember what happened to it.

The Order of Foresters, parading with their banner, was one of the many Friendly Societies that provided benefit for the sick and needy amongst their members in the days before National Insurance. In Ripley they used to meet at the White Hart and held fund raising events in Cobham Field and at Ockham Park.

Filbert Cottage near the smithy was the home of the Shoesmith family at the start of the Second World War. Mrs Rita Avery, née Shoesmith, who loaned this picture, is seen as a child standing by the front door. She, with her parents, younger brother and grandmother, had a miraculous escape when the house was destroyed by a bomb during an air raid in 1940. All were buried in the rubble but escaped unhurt. It was later rebuilt as a pair of houses.

Hurst Park Automobiles, once a showroom full of fine cars, is now the modern Miura petrol station.

Hurst House did not always have this archway through to the rear. It was the childhood home of one of Ripley's oldest residents, Mrs Ivy Sopp. Seen standing outside with her niece in the old photograph, she appears in the new picture with her nephew, Mr. Peter Shoesmith, Chairman of Ripley Parish Council. The gable-ended part of Richardson's hardware shop next door could be the second oldest domestic building in Ripley having a crown post roof typical of the mid-fifteenth century.

27

This 1920's view, (loaned by Les Bowerman) of Ripley High Street with a charabanc has changed very little, but much of the scene observed from above the Clock House Restaurant is now obscured by trees. Note the design of the early telephone box.

The smithy was at the very hub of the village and features on many of the old photographs. In this picture of around 1880 it was owned by John Pledger, members of whose family were blacksmiths in Ripley from before 1776 until 1907. He is holding the horse and the young man on his right was Walter Carter, his farrier, and grandfather of Mrs Rita Avery who loaned the picture. In recent years the smithy has been rebuilt as a modern craft shop retaining the original plan and roof layout.

One of Ripley's oldest inns, The Ship, has changed little since the early picture. Frank Clark was the landlord between 1911 and 1918. The brick front is eighteenth century concealing an earlier seventeenth century timber-framed house. The present landlords are David and Valerie Shuttle.

Ripley Post Office has been sited in a number of buildings in Ripley during its history. This location, next to the Methodist Chapel, now accommodates one of the many antique businesses in Ripley.

The Clock House Restaurant is another fine Georgian building in the High Street. It was better known as a tea room at the time of the older picture, loaned by Les Bowerman. From 1840 until 1918 it was a doctor's residence, firstly that of John King Eager and, after 1874, of Joseph Harvey Sutcliffe, in whose time it was known as Fairfield House.

The grocery tradition has been continued in Ripley by Mr Jack Richardson, who took over International Stores in 1975 when it closed after almost 60 years in the village. Before then the Tedder family had been grocers in the same shop for 50 years and prior to them the Greenfield family were also grocers in Ripley between 1826 and 1862.

HIGH STREET, RIPLEY, SURREY.

The history of this group of cottages between the Clock House and Newark Lane has been traced back to the 17th century. Although Conisbee's Corner, as it is known, is of 18th century appearance there is much evidence internally of earlier timber-framed construction.

Conisbee's corner circa 1890

The butcher's shop here has been owned by the Conisbee family since 1905 when Frederick Conisbee, a butcher in East Horsley, extended his business. Later it became a cycle shop and was the scene of a tragic fire on New Years Eve 1919/1920 when two children died.

In 1924 Frederick's son Arthur came to live here with his bride and re-opened the butcher's shop which prospers today under the ownership of his son, Peter Conisbee. Arthur is seen in the shop doorway in the lower picture.

This corner has housed a bakery at least since 1851 when William Nash is recorded as a baker; Maurice Collins was here between 1913 and 1938. It is possible that the association is much older since it is fairly certain that the corner was known, in the 17th century, as the "Frame Plott" and a document of 1699 associates this with a baker and a miller. Originally a frame plot would have been a yard where timber frames for new houses were fabricated prior to assembly on the final site.

Around the corner from the High Street into Rose Lane, these early photographs show the bakery owned by Geales. Various members of this family were here from 1853 until 1911. After the top picture was taken the grocers next door was refronted and given projecting bay windows upstairs. (see opposite page)

This photograph of Mr. Geoff Pinnock, taken in 1936, on his 500cc Ariel "Red Hunter" motorcycle also shows another view of the bakery and the cottages once known as Gamlins.

This row of cottages in Rose Lane was once known as Gamlins and was the site of another smithy in the nineteenth century. It was also the Post Office at one time. After demolition in the 1960s, a doctor's surgery was built on part of the site.

More changes have taken place in Rose Lane where the British Legion Club now occupies an earlier infants school. The weatherboarded houses on the right were demolished to make way for the entrance to White Hart Meadows.

Known as Ripley Court since circa 1840, a school was founded here by Mr. and Mrs. R.M. Pearce in 1893. The earliest documents identifying the site of the house are in the 16th century Manorial Court Rolls. John Chatfield, who was Steward to the Manor of Ripley and Send from 1731, lived here until his death in 1765. In mediaeval times Rose Lane was called Puklane, Pokelane and other similar variations. The house has undergone a number of changes since this photograph taken about 1860.

Fire Station, Ripley.

W.H.A.7

Early this century many small communities had their own fire service. Ripley was no exception with the station in Rose Lane built in 1911. Its use as such came to an end when the Ripley Brigade became part of the Surrey Fire Service in the 1950s.

The fire station was later used by the 1st Ripley Scout group until construction of their new building next door. The latter incorporates a Charles and Diana datebrick, July 29, 1981.

Ruth Hill, who appears in the older picture, and her parents before her, kept for many years a shop (now called Dowells) in Rose Lane.

Chapel Farm in Rose Lane was in mediaeval times associated with Newark Priory and would have been one of the most important farms in the area. Virtually none of its ancient farm buildings survive today, but at the end of this drive is the original farmhouse, a fine early sixteenth century structure. Built as an open hall, it has undergone considerable change, but enough remains of the massive timbers used in its construction to appreciate the strength of such houses and the reasons for the survival of so many of them to-day.

Newark Lane before 1900, the year Bonfield Terrace was built.
The present Rose Cottage was then part of a substantial building with crosswings at either end.
The lady standing by the gate was the grandmother of Mrs. Ivy Wilkinson who lives in Vine Cottages nearby.

These cottages in Newark Lane once constituted the Poor House of Ripley or, as described on J. Hassell's drawing of 1820, the alms-houses. Wall plaques at the front and back record the date 1738; the names of the churchwardens at the time when the church sold the property in 1892 are also just discernible on the rear plaque.

44

The Seven Stars, first mentioned in the Manor Roll of Papercourt in 1741, was rebuilt around 1928. The tenants in the old picture, Mr. and Mrs. Edward Rapson, were here between 1918 and 1938. Rodney and Rita Dean are the landlords today.

A mill probably existed on this site by the River Wey between Ripley and Pyrford in Saxon times; certainly a mill is recorded in the Domesday Survey of 1086. In the thirteenth century Alice de Sende granted the mill to the Priory from whom it passed to Sir Anthony Browne after the Dissolution. This building was constructed early in the nineteenth century.

Flour milling continued until 1936 after which time only animal feeds were produced. The working life of the mill came to an end in 1942 after the machinery suffered severe damage caused by builders debris in the mill stream.

In December 1966 the mill was totally destroyed by fire; a sad end to a prominent and much loved landmark. Ironically the mill escaped this fate one night during the Second World War when incendiary bombs fell all around but came no closer than setting fire to a coke store at Sir Jocelyn Bray's house nearby.

Newark Mill near Ripley.

Dunsborough House J. Hassel 1820.

The imposing Newark Lane Lodge to Dunsborough Park, although of Tudor appearance, was in fact built in 1939. The present Dunsborough House is believed to be of mainly 18th century origin, but the name occurs frequently in the Ripley and Send Manor Rolls, the earliest known reference being in 1545.

Ripley Green is one of the largest in England. It escaped the effects of the 1803 Inclosure Act largely because of the farren or grazing rights held by the owners of many Ripley houses. Some of these rights have been retained to this day. The Green also has important links with the history of cricket and was reputedly the scene of the public hanging of two murderers in 1742.

The pond, the result of earlier gravel extraction was long a feature of the Green. It began to dry up in 1933 after a new sewerage scheme was installed by Guildford Rural District Council. Eventually in 1957 the British Legion was responsible for creating the childrens playground in the dip and it is also now the site for the traditional Ripley Bonfire.

49

This old view of the High Street looking towards Guildford dates from the First World War and emphasises the width of the street at this point.

The shop beneath the blind on the left was that of Walter Frank Stiles, a draper and milliner between 1907 and 1927. His business is advertised on the estate agent's map at the front of this book.

Stamford House, now Sallie's Hair and Beauty Salon, was another of the Ryde House School buildings, in this case, circa 1900, the 'little boys residence.'

Next door to Stamford House, the present Ripley Post Office has undergone considerable change. It appears to have been an end-on mediaeval building with a roof similar to, and possibly contemporary with, that of Richardson's Hardware just along the High Street. However, the style of the brickwork around the upper floor window is the same as that on the Manor House, suggesting that the front dates from around 1650. The lean-to cottage on the corner of Rose Lane, also since rebuilt, now houses the Bon Appetit fish shop.

Ripley, Surrey. Centre of Village.   7.F.

The High Street at the crossroads must be among the widest in any village. The emptiness of the old scene is very different to that of the present day where the frock-coated figure, possibly the vicar, would be very much at risk.

The building now Cedar House and Tudor House, was previously the Cedar Restaurant. Opened in 1920 by Mr and Mrs Howard, it was visited by many celebrities of the time in the years that followed. From the 16th century until around 1800 it was the George Inn, documents from the 1570s having shown that the landlord then was Thomas Stanton, brother of the George Stanton who kept the Talbot. The present building is believed to date from the early part of the 17th century. At one time the Ripley and Send Manor Courts were held here.

Opposite the vicarage this 16th century timber-framed house was for many years Pinnock's Cafe, being owned by one of two unrelated Ripley families of that name. Ripley seems to have had many such tea rooms during and after the cycling era. Today this shop is the footwear business of Clifford James.

Between Tudor House and the Anchor is Ripley Vicarage, whose 18th century facade probably conceals an earlier building. It did not become used as such until around 1860, when the Rev. Charles Tate lived there, prior to which it had been a doctor's house. Earlier, the vicarage had been on the other side of the church but was demolished when the National School was built in 1847. In between times, at least one vicar, the Rev. Henry Albany Bowles, lived at Ryde House at the other end of the village.

Another of J. Hassell's watercolours of 1820 illustrates the Manor House or Hole's Cottages as it was then called. The intricate brickwork of the gables and window surrounds is typical of the Dutch style common in Surrey around 1650, but, in fact, this conceals an earlier timber-framed structure.

Another view of the High Street looking towards London, this time from a spot near the church. The pony and trap are strangely out of proportion and were probably superimposed onto this picture of an otherwise empty street. The principal Ryde House School building on the left was demolished after the school closed in the mid-1930s; the site is now occupied by Gibbs agricultural machinery business.

"The Mecca of all good cyclists" is how the Earl of Albemarle is reported to have described The Anchor towards the end of the last century, when the popularity of cycling had reached unequalled heights. On Whit Sunday of 1894 the police estimated that 20,000 cyclists passed through Kingston on their way to Ripley!!

This splendid picture of cyclists at The Anchor featured in an article entitled "The Ripley Road" in "The Cycling World Illustrated" of 1896, being an account of the journey by bicycle along the famous "short ten miles" from the Angel at Ditton to The Anchor. The latter had become well established in the late 1870s under its landlady, Mrs. Harriet Dibble, as a welcoming refuge for the "mud-be-spattered" cyclist. The photograph, taken nine years after Mrs Dibble's death, shows her daughter, Harriet, in the centre flanked on the left and right by her brothers Alf and Bert respectively. On the far left, adopting a typical pose of the time of studied nonchalance, is Mr. T.S. Adcock of Chichester evidently a hard-rider up for the day. The lady on the front of the tandem, Mrs Coles-Webb, is noteworthy for her "rational dress", considered very daring and even scandalous by many at the time.

The Anchor consists principally of what may be a small hall house of the early 16th century in the centre, with later crosswings on either side. It had a plastered exterior for most of the 19th century, as the 1896 photograph and the 1820 J. Hassell watercolour show. It is only comparatively recently that the timber-frame has been re-exposed.

The house next door to the Anchor was also connected with the cycling era. William Skelton established himself here as a cycle repairer in the 1880s. He apparently saw a better future in catering for the cyclists' inner needs for, by 1895, he had become a "refreshment contractor" at "The Cyclists' Rest".

Later becoming known as the Rio Cafe, the building was turned over to industrial use in the last war as Ford's Leather Works. Eventually the present electrical business moved here in the 1960s.

St. Mary's Church possesses a fine Norman chancel, circa 1160. The nave, probably thirteenth century, was rebuilt in 1846 with a small south aisle which was enlarged in 1869. The Rev. C.R. Tate, vicar between 1852 and 1874, produced the charming drawing for a letter heading, showing the church prior to 1869 and the National School adjoining. The school, designed by Henry Woodyer, was built in 1847 for £420 and served both villages until Send built its own school in 1854. Closed in 1972, it was demolished nine years later to make way for these new houses which are named Church Row. Some of the old school bricks were used to build the new boundary walls.

61

The view of Ripley when entering from Guildford at the turn of the century was very open. On the right only the police station, the school and the church were there. On the left was Toby Cottage, beyond was St. George's Farm and barn and then Perseverance Cottages. Today the site of the barn is the car park for the village hall. Toby Cottage has been a restaurant for over 60 years.

Further along the Portsmouth Road, the houses on the left had just been built at the time this photograph was taken in 1912. The AA patrol man in the picture, whose name was Curtis, lived in the first house.

The veteran car is believed to have been a French 1909 Lorraine Dietrich. The steam roller was made by Aveling & Porter of Rochester.

The spot is dominated today by the timber greenhouse and shed business founded by P.G. Barrett in 1932.

Methold Engineering opened for business on Easter weekend 1927 as the Mid-Surrey Service Station. It was founded by Mrs Sybil Methold, joined shortly afterwards by her husband, to meet the growing needs of the motorist on the busy Portsmouth Road.

Insistent that the new garage should blend harmoniously with the countryside, Mrs Methold had the petrol pumps painted a special shade of green matched with lichen from a nearby oak tree. The garage colour scheme remained thus until quite recently despite periodic protests by the petrol companies.

The business is run today by Mrs Methold's son Ken Methold and grandsons David and Chrisopher.

There has been an inn here named The Jovial Sailor, or Jolly Sailor as it was at one time, for over 200 years. The earliest reference is in a deed of 1781. The importance of Ripley's inns to seafaring travellers since Tudor times, is signified by the fact that three of them have nautical names.

The building was much altered and modernised in 1978. The part of the bar area on the left was originally stabling.

Just beyond the inn towards Guildford once stood the Ripley Turnpike where tolls were levied to pay for the upkeep of the Portsmouth Road.

Pipers Cottage is one of a small group of houses at Grove Heath half a mile to the south of Ripley. The main part was built as an end smoke-bay house and dates from around 1600.

In the early part of this century the Brown family lived there. The lady on the right was the grandmother of Mr. Roger Brown, who lives in Rose Lane today. The girl in the straw hat, his Aunt Betty, is aged 93 at the time of writing.

Originally established in the 1930s by a Mr Fisher who specialised in setting up garages and then selling them as going concerns, Fishers was bought by A.P. Hamilton a few years later. The late John Edden, who had previously been a nursery-man in Kiln Lane, joined him in 1938.

Like many other garages, the Second World War saw them engaged in a variety of tasks assisting the war effort, although they were also able to keep their motor repair work going.

Mr Edden became the sole owner in the early 1950s and retired some 30 years later. The business, today managed by David and Paul Benzimra, has been redeveloped as a modern car show room.

The Saddlers Arms in Send Marsh appears as a beerhouse in 1878 when, in Kelly's Directory, James Broomfield is listed as a beer retailer, saddler and blacking manufacturer of Cooks Green (the nineteenth century name for this spot). There are earlier references in 1816 to a smith's and saddler's shop. The property was purchased in 1914 by the Guildford brewers, Friary Holroyd and Healey, for £1500.

Bernard McLaughlin took over the tenancy around 1909 and used the adjoining land as a market garden. His granddaughter, Mrs Margaret Meech, pictured with him below as a small girl helping with the hay making, recalls the beerhouse offering accommodation and the shed at the side being used as a tea room.

After his father's death, Jack McLaughlin took over the tenancy in 1938. Shortly after the war he started the annual pumpkin competition which is still held in early October by the present landlady, Mrs Rosa Clay. With the entries displayed in the public bar, the event is concluded with a small celebration including pumpkin pie, to honour the winning specimen and aid charity.

Plowsers Estate, Send Marsh.

Manor Road in Send Marsh was originally known as Plowsers Estate. It was laid out by Mrs. Boyle of Send Manor in 1912 for self-build plot owners. Plowsers was the field name of the site according to the 1843 Tithe Apportionment.

On the corner of Send Marsh Green the timber-framed April Cottage is another sixteenth century end smoke-bay house. The smoke-bay was a transitional arrangement before the introduction of brick chimneys. The house contrasts with its modern neighbour which was previously a general store. Before the latter was built there was a shop owned by Mr and Mrs Collins in Corner Cottage just opposite (not in these pictures.)

Like its namesake in Ripley, the Manor House (also known as Send Manor) on Send Marsh Green has no manorial associations, having been known by this name only since the nineteenth century. The front part, of fine brick construction, dates from approximately 1700, although the rear of the house is Victorian.

The Send horse bus, seen here outside the Manor House, plied between Mays Corner and Woking Station at the time of the First World War. Carrying about ten passengers, the owner for much of its service was Sidney Brown.

These old cottages on Send Marsh Green originally housed farm workers on the Boughton Hall estate. They were demolished in the 1950s, the modern bungalows being built in their place.

Aldertons Farm in Send Marsh Road has been known by various names during its history. It was Mitchell's Farm in the early part of this century and members of this family are to be seen in front of the house. They lived here for over forty years until around 1922. Kelly's Directory shows Mrs Agnes Mitchell as the farmer for nearly half that time.

Boughton Hall, now a private hotel, was formerly the home of the Boughton family, prominent in the affairs of Send over a period of at least 300 years. The present house is mainly Victorian but contains parts of an earlier house. At the time of the old photograph (circa 1880) there was direct access to the Portsmouth Road at Burnt Common crossroads. A carriage-way led from behind the house, which was then the front, roughly following the present footpath to the Pathway where there was a lodge.

Although Goodgrove with its gothic style windows seems to be Victorian, it is, in fact, an old timber-framed house of the mid-sixteenth century. At the time of the old picture, circa 1900, it was three cottages, but part was later demolished leaving the present building which is one house. Goodgrove was for nearly 100 years the home of the French family, the last tenant, Mr Jim French, having lived here all his life until

his death aged 89, in 1979. The old gentleman on the left of the group, wearing an apron, was his father, who, from 1875 to 1884, was butler at Woodhill to Miss Wood and later to Lady Wharncliffe.

Send – Ripley Road.   7.K.

At this point in Send Marsh Road near the Keep House, there was a ford where the stream crossed the road. Older residents can recall paddling here as children and having to scrape the leeches off their feet afterwards! Send Post Office, run by Mr. Charles Tice, was just across the footbridge. Visible then in the distance were the early houses on Send Hill.

Looking east along Send Barns Lane from Mays Corner the right hand side is now changed with the disappearance of the trees and the hedgerow. Just visible, on the extreme left, are Box and Holly Cottages demolished with unseemly speed in 1978. The Victorian letter-box at the end of Send Marsh Road, of a standard design produced over many years, was probably made around 1890.

The Walnut Tree Garage was named after the tree which stood on the forecourt until the early 1970s. Previously this was the site of the village smithy, owned for nearly 70 years by the Sex family. The tree in front of the old building is believed to be the original.

Mr C.H. Sex came to Send from Compton in 1899 and his sons Arthur and Ron followed him into the business. It finally closed in the late 1960s after Ron's retirement.

C.H. Sex

Arthur E. Sex

Ronald C. Sex

They specialized in ornamental ironwork and many examples of this work are to be found, providing lasting tributes to their skills.

The store in Send Road, which is also the Post Office, was built in 1907 by Thomas Lucas. He lived in Send Hill at Sandmore and had previously established a successful grocers and drapery business in Ripley where Town and Country Cars is today.

He sold out to the Surrey Trading Co. who ran the business in Send with a succession of managers until 1922. Amongst these was the Dixon family, whose son Fred was later headmaster of Ripley School for 25 years.

John Dedman, who in his youth had been apprenticed with two of his brothers to Mr. Lucas in Ripley, bought the store in 1928. He ran it until 1953 with his son Ken and two daughters, Jessie and Kathleen (their initials were the J & K in the family name over the shop).

Tannery Lane, Send, with the Tannery chimneys in the background.

Members of the Womens Land Army, formed in June 1939, were a familiar sight during the Second World War as the men left to serve in the armed forces. Many came from city areas and were accommodated in billets or private houses to be near their work. After the war, some stayed on for a while; others married and settled in the area. Two of the latter are Doris Pullen and Joan Styles. They are pictured (Doris on the left) with the horses Captain and Senator in 1948 on A.W. Secrett's land at Heath Farm in Tannery Lane.

Send Tannery & Bridge, Woking

The Tannery pictured here from across the Wey Navigation by the footbridge, dates back at least to the early eighteenth century. An entry in the Ripley and Send Court Baron held on 26 April 1717 refers to "all that tanyard lately made". The old Tannery House appeared to be eighteenth century but may have concealed an earlier building; it was demolished in the 1970s to make way for the present office building.

Tannery Bridge, Send

Papercourt Farm Cottages in Tannery Lane, at the time of writing being renovated and modernised, are believed to have been the mediaeval Manor House of Papeworth or Papercourt. Although parts of the building are possibly earlier the external brickwork is likely to be mid-seventeenth century, the curved shoulders of the window lintels being similar to those of the Manor House in Ripley.

SANDY LANE.
SEND.

Until the Second World War these were the only houses in Sandy Lane. The wall on the left on the corner of Farm Lane enclosed a large Victorian house known since 1900 as The Poplars. A family named Sedgeley were among the early owners and Canning-Cookes were the last. The house and grounds were sold in the 1950s for redevelopment for just £2000. All that remains is the old coach house now in the garden of the furthest of the modern bungalows which replaced The Poplars.

Send Service Garage on the corner of Tannery Lane was founded in 1929 by Bill Challen. Since his death in 1974, his son Raymond has continued to run the business. The forecourt was reconstructed with this modern canopy in 1980.

The site of Send Service Garage was previously a chicken run in the garden of Jack Sale, Mrs. Challon's father. His house just behind, No. 91, Send Road, was formerly known as Mabbin's Cottage and is now Raymond Challen's home.

Looking westwards (circa 1910) along Send Road the houses are much the same today. On the left, the recreation ground was not established until after the First World War when prisoners of war held at Boughton Hall were employed on its preparation. The monument near the corner of Sandy Lane commemorates the opening of the ground in 1920 as a war memorial.

The completion of the Church Room in Send Road in 1894, provided, amongst other benefits, an alternative to Send Church for services on dark winter nights. The remoteness of the church from the village, according to Send Parish Magazine, had led to "previous excuses for absence" which "will now be tested".

Extensive alterations to the building in 1983 included the insertion of an upper floor in the main hall.

Send Institute, later the Drill Hall and now Lancaster Hall was endowed by Arthur Henry Lancaster and built by Charles Tice in 1911. The Institute, started in 1885 in the Uncle Tom's Cabin public house (formerly at 204 - 206 Send Road) and later moved to 85 - 86 Send Road, was part of a national movement to establish further education.

Send Ward Fire Service was formed following a parish meeting held 26 June 1913. This photograph was taken in 1914 possibly after 6 October when it was decided to move the fire station from Mr Tice's field to a building next to the Drill Hall. Left to right are: Joe Baigent, Reuben Sale, Sam Brown, W. Grove (chief officer), Frank Grove, Monty Burrows and Law Mobsby. Responsibility for Send fire services was transferred to Guildford Corporation in 1934.

The New Inn has been a public house at least since 1843 when it was shown as an inn on the Tithe Apportionment. At one time the single storey part of the building here was used as a mortuary.

Looking eastwards at Cartbridge the principal landmark, apart from the New Inn, is the shop on the corner of Potters Lane. Now Quilter Cave Ltd., it will be remembered by most Send residents as Lemons or Gladdings Stores. Until shortly before the Second World War, however, it had been, for over 67 years, a bakery, general store and, also for part of this time, a post office run by the Webb family.

Cartbridge. Send.

The bridge over the Wey Navigation at Cartbridge was a wooden one until 1915 when it was replaced by the present steel and concrete structure.

The Lock, Cartbridge.

A short distance up the River Wey from Worsfold Gates, Portmore Bridge, from which this view was taken, has now gone. A prominent landmark here is the old carpenter's workshop and smithy. Now largely disused, it is believed to date from the opening of the Navigation in 1653.

The old Broadmead Bridge was a timber structure on timber piles prior to its replacement, in 1915, by the present single span reinforced concrete bridge. Before acceptance, the latter was exhaustively tested using three steam rollers.

In 1873 the bridge was the scene of this spectacular accident when a traction engine towing a threshing machine crashed through the roadway. Three men died. Although the bridge structure was declared unsafe, it was repaired and lasted another 42 years.

The view above of the 12th century church of St. Mary the Virgin, Send, is reproduced from a watercolour by H. Petrie dated 1804. It is the earliest known accurate picture of this church and when compared with the modern photograph there is little change. Since 1804 the church yard has been extended, the lych-gate constructed and the roof repaired several times. Internally a number of changes have taken place but this charming building still preserves much of interest that the visitor might expect.

Send Grove, next to Send Church was built around 1760, possibly on the site of an earlier building. The latter may have succeeded the sixteenth century hall house, vacated since about 1600, still standing nearby. Send Grove was the home of Lt. General William Evelyn, a great grandson of John Evelyn the diarist. William died in 1783.

This drawing reproduced from E. Hassell's 1827 watercolour shows that a parapet has since been added, possibly to improve the accommodation of the second floor. The house otherwise is much the same.